850

Y0-CAV-493

Chicago in the 1920s – no bars, no gambling dens, no "booze" – by law. For this was the amazing era of Prohibition, when alcohol was outlawed throughout the entire U.S.A. Thirsty America, spurning the soda shops, turned to the bootlegger for help.

It was largely out of this that Al Capone, immigrant, bootlegger extraordinary, murderer, built his vast empire of crime. "Kill or be killed" was the creed of gangdom, and Capone stuck to it to the letter, until he was "mayor, governor and machine boss all rolled into one."

How was it possible? In this new *History Makers* title, Mary Letts gives a highly readable account of Capone's life against the background of political and police corruption rife in Chicago at the time. In a city where witnesses to crimes would mysteriously lose their memories overnight, where policemen readily accepted hush-money, where the mayor himself openly defied the law, Capone was allowed to make a brutal piece of history.

The story does not end with his death. Capone left a legacy. He taught his successors how to turn crime into big business. And, regrettably, he taught them well.

WAYLAND HISTORY MAKERS

Al Capone

Mary Letts

WAYLAND PUBLISHERS

More Wayland History Makers

The Last Czar W. H. C. Smith
Stalin F. H. Gregory & David Hayes
Goering F. H. Gregory
Martin Luther King Patricia Baker
Karl Marx Caroline Seaward
Lenin Lionel Kochan
Cecil Rhodes Neil Bates
Hitler Matthew Holden
The Wright Brothers Russell Ash
Jomo Kenyatta Julian Friedmann
Rommel F. H. Gregory
Franco Richard Kisch
Picasso David Sweetman
Bismark Richard Kisch
Captain Scott David Sweetman
The Krupps Mary Letts
Mao Tse-tung Hugh Purcell
The Borgias David Sweetman

B
Cap

1. Capone, Alphonse, 1899–1947

frontispiece: U.S. Government agents
destroying playing cards outside a gambling
den. Part of America's big "clean up"
campaign during the Prohibition era.

SBN 85340 343 0

Third impression 1977

Copyright © 1974 by Wayland (Publishers) Ltd
49 Lansdowne Place, Hove, East Sussex BN3 1HF
Printed by Page Bros (Norwich) Ltd, Norwich, England

E.B. 3/6/80

Contents

List of Illustrations

1. America — Land of Hope

At the end of the last century many of the poorer families of Europe thought of America as a land where "the streets were paved with gold." The railroads had been built, an industrial boom was on; if only they crossed the Atlantic, they told themselves, their fortunes would be made.

Gabriel and Teresa Caponi were believers in this dream. In 1893 they sold their grocer's shop in Castel Amara, a little coastal town between Rome and Naples, in Italy. They obtained immigration visas, and set out for New York.

But it was not as they had forseen. They were simply another immigrant family swallowed up in the great European exodus. They were just tradespeople without any particular skill; they spoke only Italian and were bewildered by an unknown city that was far from friendly. American sociologists had already decided that "the Italian is by nature criminally inclined" – not an attitude likely to make things any easier for them!

So they settled humbly in the slums of the Italian quarter of Brooklyn. Here the rent was about $3 per month for a room, and the families would try to squeeze as many into a room as possible. There was no hot water and there were no bathrooms. Ancient pot-bellied stoves gave out the only supply of heat. The immigrants tended to stay in their racial groups; there was the

> "We were poor, but American poor not European poor. That meant we didn't have a car, but we ate well enough." *Nelson Algren: a City on the Make.*

Opposite **The Statue of Liberty, New York, 1883.**

9

Above **"Entering a new world." Jewish immigrants to America, 1892.**

"If the child conforms to the American definition he is a delinquent in the eyes of the family. If he conforms to the family definition he is a delinquent in the eyes of the American law." *Harvey Zorbaugh; The Gold Coast and the Slum: a Sociological Study of Chicago's Near North Side.*

Italian quarter, the Irish quarter, the Polish quarter and so on. But these were always in the slum areas of the cities, and life seemed much rosier for the native-born American citizen.

Gabriel Caponi tried his luck first as a grocer, then as a barber, but the fortune he had hoped for was beyond his reach. Money became scarcer as the family grew – eventually to a total of seven sons and two daughters. Teresa had to stay up all night dressmaking in order to earn a little extra.

Alphonso was their fourth son, born in 1899. His childhood was typical of the neighbourhood. The Italian quarter was gloomy and overcrowded; the tall apartment blocks shut out the light and the streets were narrow and always full of litter. There were no parks, nowhere for children to play – so they formed street gangs and roamed the alleyways, sometimes breaking into shops or parked lorries and pilfering whatever they found. Al was tough and stocky, and feared by rival gangs when it came to fist-fighting.

His parents worked desperately hard and obeyed the law, but their life was drab, and even feeding the children was a constant struggle. The heroes of that area were quite another type. To survive in the dockland of New York, where sailors piled ashore and the streets were lined with gambling dives, tattooing parlours, liquor stores, pawnshops and prostitutes, you had to be very tough indeed.

John Torrio was just such a man. He owned a social club in the street where Al lived, and earned large sums of money by doing "services" for people. These included putting pressure on businessmen (often by bribery), rigging the results in local elections, and even arranging "accidental" deaths for a slightly higher fee. By comparison with the sinister activities of men such as Torrio, the childhood scraps of Al and his friends

Above **Brooklyn Bridge, 1883.**

amounted to nothing.

But they were influenced by Torrio nonetheless; they admired him, they tried to model their gangs on his. The grown-up gangs actually paid children to steal ballot boxes, keep watch on the streets and threaten voters at local election time. Torrio's influence on Al was probably the most powerful single influence in his life.

2. Al Capone Grows Up

When Al was fourteen he began to skip school. He still found reading difficult, and since he only spoke Italian at home his English left much to be desired. He found lessons deadly boring. One day he hit out at a teacher who was scolding him; for this he was soundly thrashed by the principal, and he ran straight out of the school gates never to return.

He went to work to earn money for the family. He may have admired Torrio more than his father, but this did nothing to affect his deep feelings of loyalty. Like most Italians he would do anything for his family. His first jobs were ordinary, and legal. He worked as a clerk in a sweet shop, a pinball setter in a bowling alley, and later a paper and cloth cutter in a book bindery.

In the evenings he would hang out on the streets looking for trouble, or sometimes – a strange contrast – listen to the old organ grinder and "Signor Tutino Giovanni, Dramatic Tenor" performing Verdi operas. His love for the opera never left him. Even at the height of his gangster career he would go to first nights surrounded by a bodyguard of henchmen dressed in dinner jackets!

When he was seventeen America entered the First World War, and Al was immediately called to join the army. He later boasted of grand exploits in the battlefield, swearing that the scar which disfigured his left

"The typical immigrant father puts on the pressure, alternately punishing the child whose low marks in school suggest that he is not going to be a successful American, and berating him for his American ways and his disrespect for his father and his father's friends from the old country." *Margaret Mead. The American Character.*

Opposite **The Bowery, New York.**

cheek was the result of flying shrapnel. Under oath at his trial, however, he finally admitted, "I was certified in the draft but never called." The scar? – the result of a knife fight in a New York saloon. What he did bring back from army service was a knowledge of modern weaponry; later in Chicago he made good use of his Sergeant's advice: "One man with a machine gun is master of fifty men with rifles and revolvers."

In 1918 at a party in one of the local cellar clubs he met a tall slim girl with fair hair. Al fell in love at first sight. The fact that Mae Coughlin was Irish, and twenty-one – two years older than him – did not put him off at all. He was so eager to be married that he obtained a special dispensation from the Church and their wedding took place immediately, on 18th December, 1918. The difference in their ages obviously worried them a little, for on their marriage certificate they both pretended to be twenty! A year later their son was born, christened Albert Francis but always known as Sonny. His godfather was none other than John Torrio.

By this time Al's leisure hours had taken a rougher turn, and he always carried a gun. He had joined a vicious gang known as the Five Pointers, a murderous bunch who controlled a large sector of New York between Broadway and the Bowery. Al was thick-set and fast moving, like a boxer in perfect physical condition, and he enjoyed violence for its own sake. Except to his close friends and his family, he was not a nice person to know.

In 1920 he was given a job as dish-washer and part-time bartender at the Coney Island Cabaret (later renamed the Harvard Inn to sound more respectable). It was owned by Frank Yale, the New York head of the Unione Siciliana (a Sicilian organization originally meant to be no more than a social pressure group, but

which soon became a force in the criminal world).
Yale was the liquor boss of New York, and his cabaret
was a meeting place for the underworld. So the job,
though hardly glorious in itself, was Al's first entry into
the life of the hardened professional criminal. Whenever quarrels broke out he was always asked to help,
which he did by the simple method of "bouncing"
(forcibly removing) the offending customer!

Al was beginning to feel restless in New York. He was
ambitious, he wanted Mae to wear furs and jewellery
and Sonny to have the education he had been deprived
of, but he was still earning a miserable wage. Also he
had already been suspected of two murders, and faced
indictment for a third if the victim, then on the hospital
danger list, should die. He did not wait to find out. A
message had come from Torrio to join him in Chicago,
and Al did not hesistate for a moment. He had now
entered the world of the full-time gangster.

Above **John Torrio.**

3. Chicago

When Capone arrived in Chicago with Mae and Sonny he found that the job waiting for him differed little from the one he had left – chief bouncer in one of Torrio's chain of brothels. But his disappointment was short-lived, for Torrio was impressed with him and soon promoted him to Manager of the "Four Deuces." This was a huge emporium of vice, a four storey building separated into saloon rooms, gambling rooms and boudoirs for the prostitutes. It was nicknamed the Four Deuces because of its address at 2222 South Wabash Avenue.

Vice was Chicago's growth industry, and Torrio was fast becoming the most powerful vice king. He not only controlled a chunk of the red light district, but he had cleverly anticipated the importance of the motor car and the new highways – Torrio roadhouses were springing up all over the State of Illinois. His yearly profits had reached $100,000 and he generously gave Capone a quarter share of this. After his dishwasher's wage of $25 a week Capone could hardly believe his luck.

Occasionally the Chicago authorities launched a clean-up campaign, but the public wanted the brothels to stay. All that happened was that a few brothels closed, and then opened up again in another street. The police were badly paid and easy to bribe, so

> "Who, me? Why, I'm a respectable businessman. I'm a secondhand furniture dealer. I'm no gangster. I don't know this fellow Torrio. I haven't anything to do with the Four Deuces. Anyway I was out of town the day Howard was bumped off. You had better do your talking to my lawyer." *Al Capone's statement to the police when questioned over the murder of Joe Howard.*

Opposite **Michigan Avenue, Chicago.**

> *"Bootlegger:* **Dealer or distributor in contraband liquor. Most likely derives from boot-leg, the upper part of a high boot (1634), in which flat bottles could be smuggled. The origin of the present use has been placed as far back as Colonial days."**
> *Dictionary definition.*

Below **State Troopers unloading captured liquor.**

Torrio's trade was rarely affected.

Just to be safe, however, Capone arranged a business alibi for himself. He printed cards bearing the words: "Alphonse Capone, **Second-hand Furniture Dealer,** 2220 South Wabash Avenue." Then he cunningly filled the corner window of his office with his "stock," – old oak tables, a piano, a rocking chair, some rugs and a shelf of books, prominent among them a family Bible.

Now that he at last had money, he could help the members of his family who were still living in the slums of New York. His mother (his father had died), four brothers and his little sister, Mafalda, came to share his house in Chicago.

The path of the new Torrio/Capone organization

had been decided by a major political event. On 17th January, 1920, the Volstead Act was passed by the United States government. This was popularly known as the Prohibition Law. Its purpose was to prohibit the sale of alcohol in order to cut down crime throughout the U.S.A. Now Chicago had voted heavily against this law, so it was obvious that there would be an eager market for liquor. Selling illegal alcohol was called bootlegging, and just about every gang in Chicago turned their attention to this new gold mine.

Torrio was a diplomatist: he forsaw the dangers of rivalry between the gangs, and he realized that with proper organization there was enough for many fortunes to be made. So he split Chicago into sections, each to be the territory of a different gang, and made profit-sharing agreements between them. The gangs were protected, but for the small-time operator it was another story – he was to be mercilessly wiped out.

Capone was made responsible for the smooth running of this plan. He was still crude and unpolished, still the roughneck from the New York slums, but he was carefully watching his boss, Torrio – and learning fast. Once, though, he carelessly attracted police attention when he lost his temper with a taxi driver and brandished his gun in the air; he was charged with drunken driving and carrying concealed weapons – both serious offences. But Torrio's bribery came to his rescue, and the charges against him were quietly dropped.

Again, when small-timer Joe Howard was shot dead after boasting how he had hijacked a truckload of Torrio/Capone beer, all the evidence pointed to Capone. In fact he was almost certainly guilty, but the case against him set the pattern for all the future gang killings. Somehow, overnight, every witness lost his memory, the inquest revealed nothing, and the prosecution had to drop its case in bewilderment.

"We, the jury, find that Joe Howard came to his death on the premises at 2300 South Wabash Avenue, from haemorrhage and shock due to bullet wounds ... said bullets being fired from a revolver or revolvers in the hand or hands of one or more unknown, white male persons ..." *Official verdict of the Joe Howard inquest.*

Below **A New York woman wearing a "rummy apron," popular during the Prohibition era.**

4. The Rout of the Old-Style Gangsters

When Torrio made his division of gang territory he left out an Irish gang called the South Side O'Donnells, because their leader, Spike O'Donnell, was then in jail.

Shortly afterwards Spike was freed on parole, and he quickly mustered his gang and began to poach in someone else's area. He undercut the price of liquor agreed by Torrio and Capone, and because his beer was less diluted than theirs he stole many customers away. Those that showed reluctance to buying from a new source were easily convinced by a flying fist or two, or the sight of revolvers bulging from the hip pockets of O'Donnell's men.

However, a certain bartender called Jacob Geis was more obstinate; Capone was his friend and he would continue to buy from him. So one evening three O'Donnell brothers, together with three of Spike's fellow prisoners (Meeghan, O'Connor and Butcher) brutally attacked him in his own saloon. He spent several weeks in hospital suffering from a fractured skull.

Capone never let a friend suffer in silence. The very next day O'Connor was shot dead, and ten days later Meeghan and Butcher were killed in their car by a fusilade of bullets from a green car which drew up alongside. If Capone was not in the car himself the orders

"The gang had a real structure. It was impossible to enforce its rules through the courts, so it created its own enforcement agency. They were living in an illegal and amoral order, and the most brutal and calloused became the most successful."
Lecturer from the University of Chicago.

Opposite **Spike O'Donnell.**

Above **Agents of the State Department of Revenue and policemen pour 228 gallons of captured liquor into the gutter. Atlanta, Georgia, 1933.**

must surely have come from him, but the police found no shred of evidence to implicate him.

Mayor Dever of Chicago, a supporter of Prohibition, was shocked by the double killing. He instantly revoked the licenses of two thousand soft drink parlours (most of these sold hard liquor in a back room, or sneakily under the counter), fired the local head of police, and replaced many of the lesser officials and police officers. Capone found this a momentary setback, for it was no longer clear who would take his bribes. But he was soon reorganized, for since most of the population actively wanted to drink their liquor – and that included most of the police force, too – it was obvious that he had the upper hand.

The police tried hard to hunt down the killers, but they were new to this sophisticated form of murder – a carefully planned assassination using modern weapons and a car with no licence plates. They did question Capone, but all they learned was that he was a second-hand furniture dealer and had acquired a licence to carry a gun.

Spike too was out of his depth. He felt outdated, and helpless in the face of the cold-blooded methods of these Italians. "I can whip this bird Capone with my bare fists any time he wants to step out in the open and fight like a man," he once exploded.

But Capone was no longer the rash youth from New York to be tempted by a challenge. He was using his mind now, he was ambitious far beyond the desire to win in a brawl. He had no intention of stepping out into the open. It took four more deaths for Spike to realize that he had better get away – and fast. Capone had crushed the first challenge to Torrio's leadership.

"The police will follow this case to a finish as they do all others. This guerilla war between hijackers, rum runners and illicit beer pedlars can and will be crushed. I am just as sure that this miserable traffic with its toll of human life and morals can be stamped out as I am that I am mayor, and I am not going to flinch for a minute." *Mayor Dever's statement after the murders of O'Connor, Meeghan and Butcher.*

5. The Takeover of Cicero

While Torrio was in Europe doing a grand tour of the capitals, and buying his mother a vast estate in Italy with a retinue of fifteen servants, Capone was busy in Chicago. He had an outrageous plan; he would literally take over the wealthy suburb of Cicero.

In secret conference with Ed Konvalinka, a local Republican politician, he selected all the candidates for the various posts. There would be Joseph Klenha for mayor, another "friend" as town clerk, another as town attorney, and so on. With the machinery of local government under his thumb he would have no police interference, his liquor trade could swell unchecked, and he could rule the middle class suburb of 70,000 inhabitants, with its high schools and prosperous banks, like a feudal baron of the Middle Ages. Capone found the thought irresistible.

Election day was 1st April, 1924. From early dawn the streets were patrolled by Capone gunmen, and at the polling booths armed men in slouch hats encouraged the voter to put his cross against the right name. If he refused he was pushed a little – or kidnapped until the evening when the booths were closed.

Outraged citizens appealed to Chicago for help, and the county judge hurriedly swore in an extra seventy policemen, who were rushed to Cicero by car. Throughout the afternoon the streets were filled with police cars

Opposite **A gangster car riddled by police bullets.**

shooting at gangster cars – and gangsters shooting back. By nightfall Mayor Klenha had been elected by an enormous majority, but this victory was marred for Capone by the death of his elder brother Frank, killed by a policeman's bullet. Capone ordered every saloon and gambling den to close and draw its blinds for two hours as a tribute to Frank, and he did not shave until after his brother's funeral as a sign of his grief.

Capone now had a private army of 700 men, many of whom were paroled convicts. He owned a gambling palace called The Ship, another called the Hawthorne Smoke Shop (bringing in at least $50,000 a day), the Hawthorne Kennel dog-tracks with as many as 400 greyhounds, not to mention the 160 bars open night and day for the sale of illegal drinks. Torrio and Capone were each taking $100,000 a week out of Cicero. Of this they paid $30,000 every week to the police as hush-money.

The soaring profits and the feeling of power went to Capone's head. He behaved like a ruthless despot. He would not brook any opposition, and he was prepared to kill anyone who offered it. Only his friends saw the generous side of his nature.

If this combination of kindness and brutality is hard to understand one must think of the violent climate of Chicago in the 1920s. Most of the ordinary people wanted alcohol, and only the gangsters, many of whom came from a background of poverty and violence, had so little respect for the law that they were happy to break it. Unfortunately they had a history of racial rivalry, the Irish hating the Italians, the Italians hating the Jews, and this was bound to lead to violence when they found themselves business competitors with a lot of money at stake. Moreover the world of gangdom had its own morality, which, put very bluntly, was "kill or be killed." To their friends they swore total loyalty,

Above **A poor family living in slum conditions in New York.**

and part of being loyal was being willing to avenge, so it needed but one killing for the murders and retaliations to snowball. If each gang had been on an equal footing the death toll would certainly have been much higher, but because Capone was so powerful he did in effect *control* the killing. Although he saw himself as a basically kind guy caught in the whirlwind of an unkind age, a helpless victim of the times, nothing can alter the fact that he acted brutally and that from his actions he built up a huge fortune.

The aftermath of the Cicero elections left Capone

with some problems. A government inquiry (there had been four deaths and forty woundings on election day) was started, but it soon petered out. Then he had to contend with the owner of the Hawthorne Inn, who had been there many years and owed nothing to Capone. He refused to buy Capone's beer and stood firm against threats; he was going to stay, he said, and if he left he would leave in a coffin. He did.

Capone then took over the Hawthorne Inn and made it his local headquarters. He converted the upper floor to a suite and office for himself, with bullet-proof steel shutters fitted at the windows and doors. Here he entertained the politicians of Cicero, and gave them his instructions.

If Mayor Klenha thought he was a partner of Capone he was soon made wiser. Once, when he failed to carry out one of Capone's orders, Capone met him outside the City Hall, knocked him down the steps and kicked him viciously. A policeman watched the scene calmly, and then strolled away across the street.

The character of Cicero changed from a peaceful suburb to a gangsters' town, teeming with gamblers and heavy drinkers. Capone was becoming notorious. Busloads of tourists were driven past "Capone Castle" (the Hawthorne Inn), his flashy cars were stared at in the streets, and he was easily recognizable at the race track from his flamboyant suits of sunburst yellow and vivid green. He was almost a local hero – known as "The Mayor of Crook County"!

The locals of Cicero took little notice of the change. The residential areas were safe and quiet; the only violence was in the world of gangster and politician, and the rowdy nightlife was confined to downtown Cicero. The general public really did not care.

The only person who attempted to stir them – to draw attention to Capone's ugly methods, and show

"When the cops and the prohibition agents come here after hours all the time to get drunk, why, of course, they go along with us. They always tip us off to the raids. An injunction means nothing. When the owner of a place is caught by one he opens up somewhere else under another name."
A Cicero saloon-keeper, during an interview.

them he was more than the benign provider of drink to a thirsty population – was young Robert St. John, editor and founder of the Cicero *Tribune*. He bravely chased after anti-Capone stories, and was badly beaten up for his pains. When he left hospital after a week of treatment he was surprised to find that his bill had been paid – by a Mr. A. Capone. But, arriving at his office, he discovered why; Capone had forged his signature and bought control of the *Tribune*. He was sitting at St. John's desk wreathed in smiles, and the former owner had no choice but to pack his bags and leave.

6. Capone's Business

During the summer months of 1924 the gang rivalries, which Torrio's partitioning had tried to suppress, began to break through the surface calm. The greatest rival to the Torrio/Capone organization had always been Dion O'Banion, the fiery leader of a powerful Irish gang. Torrio and Capone had tried to appease him with a share in their Cicero takings, but he returned the favour by refusing them even the smallest share of his own profits.

Capone was furious. But he listened to Torrio's advice, realizing that a confrontation would only lead to open war. He had a quick temper, and he was not such a great diplomatist as Torrio, but he had the sense to know that violence was never the best solution. Much later on, after years of bloodshed, he told a reporter: "I'm tired of gang murders and gang shootings. It's a tough life to lead. You fear death every moment, and, worse than death, you fear the rats of the game who'd run around and tell the police if you don't constantly satisfy them with money and favours."

So O'Banion, pleased to find himself unchecked, decided on more blatant provocation. He began to meddle in politics. He undermined the Democratic Party (the party which Capone supported) in the North-side wards of Chicago, and helped the Republicans win the local election. He made a great success of

> "Are we living by the code of the Dark Ages or is Chicago part of an American Commonwealth? One day we have this O'Banion slain as a result of a perfectly executed plot of assassins. It is followed by this amazing demonstration [the funeral]. In the meanwhile his followers and their rivals openly boast of what they will do in retaliation. There is no thought of the law or of the people who support the law." *Mayor Dever's statement after O'Banion's funeral.*

Opposite **Al Capone, pictured in 1932.**

his beer interests in Cicero – interests that Capone had actually *given* him, and refused to share out the money. He robbed the Sibley warehouse of $1,000,000 worth of bonded whisky, and then hoarded all the proceeds to buy himself a distillery in flagrant competition with Capone and Torrio. He even hijacked whisky from some of Capone's allies. He was becoming too successful and far too self-satisfied for Capone's peace of mind, and Capone restrained his anger with difficulty.

Then came the last straw – he double-crossed Torrio. The Sieben Brewery was owned jointly by Capone, Torrio and O'Banion, and one day O'Banion told them he wanted to sell out and retire to a quiet ranch in Colorado. He said he would hand over all the details on 19th May – he had been warned that a police raid was planned for that date.

The police were amazed at their luck; they confiscated thirteen truckloads of beer and arrested some prime gangsters, chief among them Torrio and O'Banion. O'Banion had risked arrest himself for the pleasure of trapping Torrio. Torrio was later sentenced to nine months in jail, but O'Banion was dead by the time the case came to court: it had not occurred to him that Capone might smell treachery.

Capone was set on revenge, but he had to act warily. O'Banion was Chicago's only three-gun man, and he was ambidextrous. Capone's chance came after the death of Mike Merlo, the Chicago President of the Unione Siciliana. The Italians gave Merlo a sumptuous funeral, and Capone obligingly sent the order for $100,000 worth of floral wreathes to O'Banion, whose hobby, believe it or not, was flower arrangement.

On 10th November O'Banion was shot when three men came to "collect their wreath." The police arrested Capone's ace killers, Scalise and Anselmi, but their lengthy trial ended predictably in acquittal.

The Irish gave O'Banion an even more spectacular funeral than Merlo's, and Capone steeled himself to attend. He did not dare stay away, for the only man he really feared had taken over leadership of the O'Banion gang. This was Hymie Weiss, an unemotional Pole, who had made it clear that he held Capone responsible for the murder. The violence Torrio had tried so hard to contain finally broke loose.

Below **Dion O'Banion's funeral Chicago.**

33

7. Business Competition

Hymie Weiss decided that the bitterest revenge, the way to really hurt Capone, was to attack his friends. Capone used to spend quiet evenings at the restaurant of Tony the Greek, whose T-bone steaks he would describe with shining eyes, and whose company he genuinely loved. Tony admired Capone unreservedly, and told many stories of the gangster's generosity. Apparently one rainy November evening a bedraggled boy had stumbled into the restaurant with an armful of newspapers to sell. "How many you got left, kid?" asked Capone. "About fifty, I guess," the boy answered. "Throw them on the floor then. Here," handing him a $20 note, "run along home to your mother."

One night soon after O'Banion's funeral, while Capone and Tony were talking over a meal, Tony heard some customers arrive and went downstairs. But he never returned, and his body was found later drowned in quick-lime. Capone waited anxiously, and when he was told the "customers" were Weiss's men he sobbed quite openly, too distraught to even leave the table for the whole of that night.

Hearing of Weiss's plan, Torrio fled the city, and was closely pursued by Weiss's gunmen to Arkansas, the Bahamas, out to Cuba and back again to Chicago. He might just as well have saved himself this merry dance, for he was finally gunned down outside his own

> "They were of an alley-cat breed, the inbred savagery, duplicity and insane pride of the Sicilian bandit overlaid by their training in competitive brutality in an American metropolitan slum. They carried in their pockets rosaries, crucifixes and revolvers." *Kenneth Allsop's description of the Genna brothers in The Bootleggers.*

Opposite **James Genna.**

front door. But they only succeeded in wounding him. Capone rushed to the hospital, insisting on a round-the-clock vigil at his partner's bedside. But Torrio's nerve had gone, and before serving his nine-month sentence for the Sieben raid he officially handed over the business to Capone.

So Capone was now in a very powerful but dangerous position. After narrowly missing death when Weiss's men riddled his car with machine-gun bullets, he decided to buy himself an armoured sedan. It was a V8 Cadillac, and it cost him no less than $20,000. Carefully built to his orders, it weighed seven tons and was really more a tank than a motor car. It had armour-plated body work, a steel petrol tank, windows of bullet-proof glass, a moveable back window (the rear-gunner's position!) and a loud police siren. Moreover he never moved an inch without a convoy of bodyguards behind, and a scout on a motor bike two hundred yards in front.

Capone was now set on gaining sole command of the entire bootleg industry, and this meant controlling the Unione Siciliana. It was a strictly Sicilian organization, similar to the Mafia – and it inspired feelings of pride, reverence and loyalty just as strongly as any religion. Its 15,000 members were a formidable force. Capone knew that he, a mere Italian, could never be President of the Unione, but he intended to have a friend in that position.

The six Genna brothers thought otherwise. Originally allies of Capone, the Presidency held for them the magic attraction of gold. But they knew that they were not Capone's choice. The Gennas had grown rich and powerful through control of the "alky-cooking" business. They had hit upon the idea of importing poor Sicilian families, and giving each a little flat equipped with an alcohol still. The man of the house was paid

$15 a day just to keep the still stoked, and to strain off the sugar corn liquid. Then the raw alcohol was collected each week and taken to the Genna warehouse. Naturally they could boast the support of most of the Sicilian community.

Before Capone had time to think they had declared Angelo Genna the new President. But Capone had a rare stroke of luck – Hymie Weiss arranged the killing of Angelo in May, 1925, and a policeman shot Mike Genna in June. Unable to rely on his enemies to continue helping in this way, Capone himself ordered the death of Tony Genna in July.

The strength of the Genna family had been broken, and the three remaining brothers needed no more convincing – without a moment's delay they fled Chicago.

Below **Angelo Genna's funeral.**

8. Who Killed McSwiggin?

Although most of Capone's activities were blatantly illegal – alcohol distilling, owning saloons, selling hard liquor, prostitution, murder, bribery . . . he rarely had to worry about legal interference. Scores of policemen and Prohibition agents were on his payroll, and his generous handouts to political funds gave the authorities good reason to leave him alone.

The public in general did not object; those who wanted to could buy alcohol at a reasonable price and without fuss – they just had to walk into the nearest saloon. And although much of the gang violence did take place in crowded streets, city life as a whole was no less safe than it had always been. In fact, on the rare occasions when innocent passers-by were hurt, the gangster responsible would usually treat them to the finest medical treatment money could buy!

But Capone's system was not inviolate: a public outcry could easily upset it. This occurred with the murder of a young police official called McSwiggin, on 27th April, 1926. This was not a case of gangsters killing gangsters (the public did not mind about that), and it was taken as a direct attack upon the State.

Awakening from their lethargy, the heads of the legal departments were galvanized into action. "It will be war to the hilt against these gangsters!" cried State Attorney Crowe. But his challenge blew away in the

> **"If a police officer detains you, even for a moment, against your will, and you kill him, you are not guilty of murder. It's just manslaughter. If the policeman uses force of arms, you may kill him in self-defence and the law cannot harm you."**
> *Argument used by one of Capone's lawyers during a trial.*

Opposite **William McSwiggin.**

39

wind, for although a Special Prosecutor was appointed to make the investigation, and five Special Grand Juries were impanelled in the course of it, it found out nothing of any value.

The police were more effective, however. To Capone's alarm Chief Detective Schoemaker took over the case, and he was known in the gang world as "Wily Old Shoes." He was highly conscientious. He discovered three Thompson sub-machine guns had been sold to a member of Capone's gang, that Capone, his brother Ralph and three others were seen – fully armed – on the night of the murder, and that Capone had been feuding with the North Side O'Donnell gang. Now McSwiggin had been shot while in the company of two

Right **Ralph Capone, brother of Al Capone.**

O'Donnell members (also killed), although his reason for being with the gangsters was never fully explained. In fact the police perhaps too eagerly announced that he had been "following up a case...," so embarassed were they by Capone's unruffled statement during questioning: "Why should I kill him? I paid McSwiggin, and I paid him plenty, and I got what I was paying for."

Newspaper headlines declared: "It has been established to the satisfaction of the State's Attorney's office and the Detective Bureau that Capone in person led the slayers of McSwiggin."

But Capone had disappeared. Days turned into weeks, April became May, and not until the end of July did Capone send word that he would answer the charge. He had been waiting for the public clamour to subside.

The Chief Justice dismissed the case with the words: "This complaint was made by Chief of Detectives Schoemaker on cursory information and belief." This judgment, plus the studied impotency of the State's Attorney's office to expose large-scale corruption, had a very demoralizing effect upon the police force. Even if they risked their lives to collect what seemed foolproof evidence against a gangster, he could still walk out of court a free man.

"On the whole, a review of years past gives no special occasion for alarm at the present moment. Crime in volume and type wheels and rotates in cycles ... The situation is well enough in hand to encourage the hope that there will be no outbreak on any such scale as in the recent past ..." *Part of the report compiled by the Five Special Grand Juries.*

9. The Assault Upon Cicero

The time had finally come for Weiss to take his revenge on Capone for the killing of O'Banion. He chose the sunny afternoon of 20th September, the day of the autumn meeting at the Hawthorne racetrack. It was a brazen attack, a daylight assault on Capone's headquarters in Cicero from a convoy of seven cars, all armed with Thompson sub-machine guns. As the cars drew level with the Hawthorne Hotel they came to a halt, and from their windows hailed a storm of more than a thousand bullets. The lobby and the walls of the hotel were riddled with holes, and the streets littered with broken glass. When the sound of firing died away the cars roared off, leaving behind them a scene reminiscent of wartime bombing.

Miraculously, no one was killed. Capone himself, thanks to the quick-thinking of his bodyguard, Frank Rio, had flung himself to the ground, and everyone else had followed his example. The only casualty was a Mrs. Ferguson who had come to town for the races, and was sitting in her car when the shooting began. A piece of glass had embedded itself in her eye, and Capone insisted on paying $10,000 to specialists to save her sight. He also reimbursed the shopkeepers whose shop fronts had been damaged.

Then he planned his retaliation. He knew that he was up against a man with a cold heart and a brilliant

"Hymie Weiss is dead because he was a bull-head. Forty times I've tried to arrange things so that we'd have peace in Chicago and life would be worth living. Who wants to be tagged around night and day by guards? There was, and there is, plenty of business for us all, and competition needn't be a matter of murder, anyway." *Al. Capone, in an interview with the press after Weiss's murder.*

Opposite **Al Capone, pictured in 1928.**

mind – and that he could not afford any mistakes. He also knew that the police would be watching him.

A few days later a man rented a room in the house opposite Weiss's headquarters, overlooking the front entrance, while a woman took a room facing the rear door of Weiss's office. These two then vanished, and the rooms were taken over by six men – three in each room. Their vigil lasted from 5th October until the afternoon of 11th October, for they wanted to act when there was no risk of being seen. The shooting was over in a matter of seconds, and Weiss's bullet-riddled body was found outside the front entrance of his office.

The only trace of the killers was a pile of cigarette ends – hundreds of them – lying at the feet of the chairs which stood by the windows in both rooms.

That day Capone was to be found at the Hawthorne Hotel, in shirtsleeves and house slippers. He even telephoned the Detective Bureau offering to come in for questioning, but they declined. Both Chief of Detectives Schoemaker and Chief of Police Collins were convinced that he had hired the killers, but after the McSwiggin case they knew they were powerless.

Collins even said, "It's a waste of time to arrest him. He's been in before on murder charges. He has his alibi. He was in Cicero when the shooting occurred." And there the case had to rest.

Only four men were ever recognized as "Big Shots" in Chicago gangland – Torrio, Capone, O'Banion and Weiss. Now only Capone remained. He was undisputed king. So now he could afford to show some magnaminity. He wanted peace, and he happily agreed to hold a "Robber Barons Council" at the Hotel Sherman. So on 20th October, 1926, he summoned a meeting of the main gangleaders, and drew up a treaty in the comfort of the V.I.P. suite – right there in the shadow of the City Hall, across the road from the offices of the

"I told them we were making a shooting gallery of a great business and that nobody profited by it. It's hard and dangerous work, aside from any hate at all, and when a fellow works hard at any line of business, he wants to go home and forget about it. He don't want to be afraid to sit near a window or open a door."

Al Capone in a press interview after the "Robber Barons Council."

Above **City Hall, Chicago, 1926.**

Chief of Police!

It was agreed that the killings would stop, and the gangleaders would keep the peace. Chicago was divided into areas for each gang, with Capone taking the lion's share.

Capone now controlled a nationwide operation, with supplies of liquor pouring in from New York (Frank Yale, his employer during those far-off days of poverty, was his contact there), the Canadian border, New Orleans, Cuba and the Bahamas. The Mafia bosses today might not be unduly amazed by this, but at that time it was the largest criminal organization the United States had ever known, and the most lucrative. Government investigators later estimated that Capone's annual revenue must have climbed beyond $105,000,000.

10. Capone at Home

Taking advantage of the lull in the fighting, we will take a look at the domestic side of Capone's life.

He lived in a two-storey, brick-faced house in Prairie Avenue, in the heart of a peaceful middle class neighbourhood. Here there were no gang shootings, no gambling dens, no alky-cookers – not even any Italians apart from the Capone family. It was the sort of orderly locality where tired businessmen would drive home after their day's work, certain of ease.

The Capone house was divided into two flats; one for Al, Mae and Sonny, and the other for Mama Teresa, her daughter Mafalda, and the two sons, John and Matthew. Originally there were five sons, but Frank had been killed on Cicero election day, and Ralph had moved out to his own home. Their neighbours included businessmen, a Presbyterian minister, two policemen and one Sergeant of Police – and the general opinion of the street was that the Capones were an "agreeable and civilized family."

Capone reserved his flamboyancy for his downtown life. At home he relaxed in carpet slippers and lounge-robe, listened avidly to music on the radio and played games with his adored son. The same man whose gourmet habits were described in the newspapers – six course feasts washed down with magnums of champagne – prided himself on his own spaghetti dishes, and

"I can't feel he was all-evil, like he's been painted since then. Sure he was a cold-blooded killer, but he had his good side. I see him as a victim of his time and circumstances. Capone was tolerated by the public because – let's face it – he was giving them a service they wanted."
James Doherty, Crime reporter of the Tribune.

Opposite **Al Capone's Chicago home in Prairie Avenue.**

Below Al Capone, surrounded by bodyguards, smiles as baseball star Gabby Hartnett autographs a baseball for his 12-year old son, Albert (Sonny) Capone.

would stand solemnly at the kitchen range with an apron tied around his neck. His beer, hard liquor, wine and champagne were all over Chicago, but his own cellar contained nothing but bottles of Chianti, which he announced was the "proper wine for the home."

In Capone's eyes, Mae was the ideal wife. She was angelically beautiful and very timid. She stayed quietly at home and let him lead his life without a murmur of reproach. Although he always treated her with kindness and generosity, he certainly spent many nights out on the town drinking and gambling, sometimes sleeping in his private suite at the Lexington Hotel where his young mistress had taken up permanent residence. Mae was also wonderfully discreet; she never talked to newspaper men, much to their disappointment, and she had a horror of publicity. A man in Capone's line of business could not have hoped for a finer lady.

Mafalda went to a nearby girls' high school, and just before Christmas the Capone sedan would pull up at the school entrance, jammed to the top with baskets of sweets, fruit, whole turkeys and presents for every pupil and teacher.

Capone was a great sports enthusiast, and whenever he went to boxing fights he would buy an extra $100 worth of tickets, which he gave to the most eager-looking boys in the queue. He regularly dropped $20 notes into the grubby hands of poor street-kids, and had a scale of tips that went $5 for a newsboy, $10 for a cloakroom attendant, and $100 for a waiter.

He was generous to the poor, particularly the Italian poor. In hard winters the working-class of Cicero could draw all the groceries, clothing and fuel that they needed from coal depots and department stores on the Capone account.

Of course Capone did have plenty to be generous with.

48

Some of his largesse was carefully calculated. He gave away hundreds of diamond belts and ruby-set gold cigarette cases to politicians and business associates, whose cellars were also kept well stocked with liquor. And he had to pay heavily for a lot of people's silence.

He spent lavishly on his own pleasures. More than $10,000,000 slipped away into the bookies' tills at the race-racks (he always bet for a win, and he usually lost). And he was addicted to craps and roulette. But he studiously avoided the stock market, denouncing Wall Street as a "crooked game."

Capone's taste in clothes became notorious. There were fedora hats and button-holes, diamond cuff-links and specially tailored suits in amazing colours that no-one else seemed to have thought of – lilac, apple green, mustard, primrose, chocolate brown, tangerine. An eleven-carat blue-white diamond ring glittered on his non-trigger finger – $50,000 worth.

Capone changed the image of the gangster, much to the later delight of Hollywood. Athletic youths with keen eyes and smart clothes took over from the earlier type – the furtive, sallow-faced creature, with cap pulled down over his eyes and cigarette drooping from a listless lip. Capone hired his men with great care.

Apart from sports and gambling, Capone's other great love was music. He often went to first nights, protected by an entourage of eighteen armed body-guards, and he more or less sponsored the growth of jazz. For without the bootleg industry, which kept the drink flowing and enabled the night clubs to stay open all through the 1920s, jazz would never have had an audience. Capone would often spend whole evenings in jazz dives. The gangsters identified with this music – "Jazz has got guts, it don't make you slobber."

So Capone was not only a ruthless killer and a multi-millioniare criminal, he was also an adoring father, a thoughtful husband and a generous benefactor of the poor – a strange combination indeed.

Above **The soup kitchen which Al Capone opened in 1930 in Chicago to help feed the unemployed.**

"Capone was a very smooth man. He was honourable and hardly ever made enemies. His outward speech was friendly. The idea that he founded a kind of syndicate of evil is a lot of horn-swoggle. The city was syndicated by the Anglo-Saxons who founded it – by the first guy who sold a bottle of whisky to an Indian." *Nelson Algren. Chicago, a City on the Make.*

49

c

11. The Capone Organization

Although the Cicero headquarters were at the Hawthorne Hotel, the real headquarters of the Capone organization were in the Metropole Hotel, 2300 South Michigan Avenue – the Chicagoan equivalent to New York's Fifth Avenue.

Here the gang occupied no less than fifty rooms on two heavily guarded floors. They had their own private elevators and their own private bars; every hotel regulation was flouted, and gambling went on openly day and night.

The lobby of the Metropole was a beehive of activity, especially on Sunday mornings. Prominent criminal lawyers, top police officials and politicians waited alongside scurrilous bar-owners for the honour of an audience with the big man. Policemen in uniform streamed in and out.

Capone was to be found in rooms 409 and 410, with a fine view of the boulevard. His hallway was patrolled by sentinels posted at regular intervals, and his bodyguard waited attentively in an ante room next to his suite. The room was a virtual arsenal of the latest fire-arms.

There was also a specially constructed underground vault containing $150,000 worth of wines and liquors. This was for the gang's personal use.

It was from here that Capone kept a firm hand on the

Opposite **Interior of a New York speakeasy, 1933.**

pulse of Chicago; nothing that happened in police or political affairs escaped his wary eye. He had much more than simple immunity from the law, for sometimes it was actually he who gave the orders. Once, for example, when one of his gang had been held in custody he angrily telephoned the judge:

"I thought I told you to discharge that fellow!"

"Oh, I was off the bench that day. I wrote a memo for Judge . . . and my bailiff forgot to deliver it."

"Forgot! Don't let him forget again!"

Despite the fact that he was a notorious gang leader and a disgrace to the city of Chicago, Capone was actually invited by the authorities to join the welcome party for Commander Francesco de Pinedo, the goodwill emissary of Benito Mussolini, then President of Italy. The city leaders hastily explained that it was only a safety measure – they were afraid of anti-fascist riots (Mussolini was head of the Fascist Party), and Capone's presence must surely prevent this. It was not a tribute to Capone's status, they said.

Not far from the Metropole Hotel were the smaller, more intimate offices of a "Dr. A. Brown." Like "Alphonse Capone, Second-hand Furniture Dealer," this was an expertly prepared disguise. The waiting room could have belonged to any doctor, with its comfortable chairs and the previous year's magazines piled upon the centre table. Doctor Brown even had neat rows of medicine bottles lining the shelves of one wall. These were really the stock samples of almost every known variety of liquor, and would-be customers were allowed to take them to their own chemists for analysis.

The "surgery" door led to the offices. Here a clerical staff of twenty-five were busy with ledgers, card indexes, and all the paraphernalia of an accounts department. Absolutely nothing connected with the Capone organization was overlooked, from every cent that came in from distilleries, saloons, roadhouses, hotels, speakeasies, racetracks, gambling joints and brothels, to every bit of money paid out in bribes to the police or Prohibition agents.

Here the man in charge was Jack Guzik, Capone's financial genius. Guzik was also entrusted with the national side of the organization, and kept a check on the times and details of the liquor shipments.

One day there was a state of near-panic when the record books were seized in a police raid. Mayor Dever was delighted, and said the documents would be turned over to the government. Brave words. A municipal judge impounded them, and at a special and mysteriously unpublished hearing he returned them to Capone. The United States District Attorney publicly accused the judge of a "direct refusal to co-operate with the government," but the judge did not even bother to justify himself. He was in Chicago, Capone was in Chicago, and no more need be said!

The most extraordinary figure involved in the corruption was Mayor William Hale Thompson of Chicago, otherwise known as "Big Bill the Builder." Although the law forbade alcohol, Thompson drank plentifully and openly, and his slogan for the mayorial election of 5th April, 1927, was "I'm wetter than the middle of the Atlantic Ocean." A little while later the Illinois Bar Association made an investigation into organized crime, and found that most of Mayor Thompson's campaign funds had come from a certain Mr. Capone. This was why Capone had such an easy time with the authorities, and why the public, faced with such a starkly corrupt administration, remained almost indifferent to the corrupt activities of the gangs.

"When I was Mayor I was held responsible for crime conditions, and properly so, and I accepted the responsibility without trying to shift it to the courts . . . With practically the same men as are now in the police department, I drove the crooks out of Chicago, and will do so again if I am elected Mayor." *One of Mayor Thompson's claims before the Mayorial election of April, 1927.*

12. The Siege of the Detective Bureau

Capone's peace treaty worked well until the time of the 1927 April election, when there were a few minor skirmishes. But in the background a new menace was threatening him – the last serious threat to his supremacy. After he had defeated the Genna gang he had nominated his friend, Antonio Lombardo, as President of the Unione Siciliana. Now the Aiello gang, lead by Joseph Aiello, had mustered together the broken members of the old Genna gang, the old O'Banion gang, and several freelance enemies of Capone.

The Aiellos toured the United States, canvassing support among the Sicilians against Capone. They offered blood-money amounting to $50,000 to the man who could kill him. But Capone's men were too clever for them. Between May and October, 1927, four corpses were found, and the Chicago police force could make nothing of it. The victims were all men from out of town, Sicilians by the look of them; each was clutching a silver nickel in his right hand. Robbery could not have been the motive, since their fat wallets had not been touched. In reality they were all entrants in the Aiello competition, murdered by Capone's fastest gunman, Jack McGurn.

Then the Aiellos bribed the chef of the "Little Italy" restaurant to put prussic acid in Capone's soup. But the chef was too frightened and he told Capone, who decided

"Men, the war is on. We have got to show that society and the police department, and not a bunch of dirty rats, are running this town. It is the wish of the people of Chicago that you hunt these criminals down and kill them without mercy." *Chief Detective William O'Connor's address to his Special Force after the deaths of six Aiello gang members.*

Opposite **Joseph Aiello.**

> "I am a property-owner here. I have done nothing wrong. I don't intend to do anything wrong and I don't intend to leave. The only way you can get rid of me is to have the United States Supreme Court say there is a law to put me out." *Al Capone's answer to a summons by Miami officials.*

Below **Al Capone's estate on Palm Island.**

that things had gone too far.

He increased his bodyguard to a virtual army, his gunmen reduced the Aiello gang by six, and he waited for his chance to settle the score with Joseph Aiello himself. It came on the day that Joseph was taken to the Detective Bureau for questioning. Capone swiftly ordered his men to surround the building and block off all exits. Not a shot was fired, but it was such an amazing spectacle – armed gangsters in a bristling cordon round the city's chief law enforcing agency – that it caused a general uproar. Newspapers all over the country took up the story, laughingly calling it The Siege of the Detective Bureau.

The "siege" had two main results, one of which Capone had planned, but the other he certainly had not. It did indeed terrify Aiello into a speedy retirement – he lay low for two years, after which he was killed anyway – and Capone had no more challengers. The result Capone had not forseen was the sudden hostility of the Chicago authorities. Deeply embarrassed by the national news coverage, they decided that Capone had grown too powerful and too notorious for comfort. In order to regain a little of their wounded self-respect they resolved to defeat him.

So, unknown to Capone, government agents were busily wading through his millions of financial transactions over the years after 1924, in the hope of bringing a tax evasion charge against him. But these measures would take years to bring about results, and so their immediate move was simply to make his life difficult. They watched him like a hawk.

When Capone took Mae and Sonny for a short trip to Los Angeles in December, 1927, he was greeted by the Chief of Police: "You're not wanted here. We're giving you twelve hours to leave." Surprised but obedient, they returned to Chicago and crept into their house under cover of darkness. But in the morning the police were outside. They followed him everywhere, fined him for carrying a gun, stopped him, searched him – until he decided there was no escape but to leave.

His Los Angeles experience was repeated at St. Petersburg, Miami, and New Orleans. The administration had managed to rid themselves – temporarily – of Capone, but they had also worsened their own embarassment. Capone's travels caught the popular fancy, he was called "The Man without a Country," and his wanderings were recorded by a gleeful press, lavish in its ridicule of Chicago.

Finally Capone won. Fronted by a wily real estate broker he bought a villa on Palm Island, Miami Beach. As a property owner there was nothing Florida could do to get rid of him.

Capone's house in Chicago had been modest, so in Florida he decided to indulge himself. The villa was neo-Spanish in style, gleaming white, with a green-tiled roof, fourteen spacious rooms, an enormous porch, mosaic patios, palm trees breaking the smoothness of the lawns, and finally its own private dock large enough for three sea-going craft. Capone built heavy oak gates and a high wall around the garden, and posted his bodyguard in the gatehouse (which had three adequate rooms). From here they could notify him by house phone of any visitors. He added a vast swimming pool, a two-storey boathouse, a rock pool with tropical fish and various sea-craft to fill up the dock.

Then, settling back in the Florida sun, he told journalists with a meaningful grin, "I like it here. It's warm, but not *too* warm!"

Below **Al Capone relaxing at his Palm Island home.**

13. The Pineapple Primary

It was not only the feeling of being mocked by the outside world that turned Chicago against Capone. It was also the approach of a local Primary election, in which Mayor Thompson was fighting another Republican faction for control of all the important posts. Thompson would remain Mayor, but he risked having rivals elected to posts such as Governor, State Attorney, and District Commissioner.

Mayor Thompson was caught in a trap. Being a heavy drinker he desperately wanted the bootleg industry to carry on, but he had to make a show of fighting crime. We have seen to what extent the two were inseparable.

As a politician the Mayor can only be described as a buffoon and a rascal, but as a representative of the average Chicagoan's views he was fairly typical. They were against crime and violence, but they hated Prohibition, and many of them secretly admired Capone and his brilliance in "making monkeys" of the police.

The election campaign was the most violent America had ever known. Dozens of bombs, called "pineapples," were tossed at politicians' houses, and one Thompson opponent known as Diamond Joe Esposito was murdered. The gangs were blamed, and Capone (then in Florida) was the name on everyone's lips. But the

"Deneen [Mayor Thompson's chief rival] is filling this town with dry agents [Prohibition men] from Washington, who run around like a lot of cowboys with revolvers and shotguns. Our opponents would have us believe we don't know how to run our town. Vote for the flag, the constitution, your freedom, your property, as Abraham Lincoln and William Hale Thompson would like to have you do." *From a speech by Mayor Thompson before the "Pineapple Primary."*

"Evidently the self-respect of Chicago is tired of being made a byword and a laughing stock by its present mayor." *London's Morning Post.*

Opposite **Mayor ("Big Bill") Thompson of Chicago.**

culprits were never caught.

The speeches were stormy, often degenerating into venemous personal attacks. Polling day itself was like a repeat of the 1924 Cicero election with all its kidnappings and ballot-box thefts. Capone was a conspicuous figure, returning from exile to cast his vote, and parading through Cicero to the delight of the crowds.

The result, though, was the greatest shock of all – a resounding defeat for Mayor Thompson. All his friends were ousted from office, and newspapers from all over the United States and Europe revelled in the news. To Capone's relief, however, Thompson refused to resign as Mayor: "Let's analyse the situation," he said. "I haven't lost out so much in the election. I've got a majority of the ward committee-men, and the sanitary district trustees. You'd think I'd lost the whole fight. Why should I resign?"

Capone was not unduly alarmed. The big names might have changed but the system remained the same. As Mr. Roche, chief investigator of the State Attorney's office, remarked: "A one-legged Prohibition agent could stop the beer in a day," then, pausing for a second, "if he were honest."

Yet it was a crucial political turning-point. The voters of Chicago had rebelled against corrupt government, and Capone's status would never be the same again. He still had a multi-million dollar business, which he had now expanded into one legal trade: a partnership in a cleaning and dyeing concern. But he no longer had politicians under his thumb, and the attacks against him were mounting.

He had made the fatal mistake of becoming too prominent, and publicity can kill as surely as it can create. Once he had become a cult hero, the authorities had no choice but to crush him. It would take time, but the battle had at last begun.

"O Thou that didst care for Nineveh . . . and Thou that didst weep over Jerusalem, dost Thou still brood over these modern cities? We pray thee to rule over Chicago – this young and strong, good and bad, city – and out of man's worst, bring Thine own best." *Pre-election prayer by Rev. John Thompson of the Chicago Methodist Temple.*

"The political revolution in Chicago came as a surprise to most political observers. They had thought that the city was disgraced, but not ashamed." *New York Times.*

Opposite **Al Capone.**

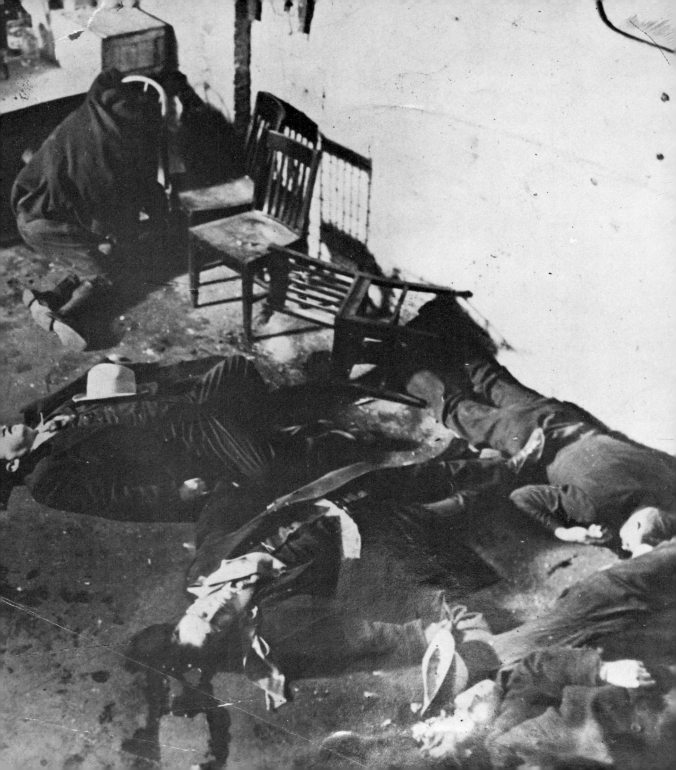

14. The St. Valentine's Day Massacre

Capone followed the morality of gangdom. He was always faultlessly loyal to a friend, and utterly ruthless if that friend betrayed him. This chapter shows how unswerving the gang world was in executing its own cruel brand of justice.

Back in 1926 Capone had organized his national network for the bootleg industry, linking up with gangs with amazing names – Egan's Rats of St. Louis, the Purple Gang of Detroit, and Max Boo-Boo Hoff of Atlantic City and New Jersey. His own men were in charge of Florida and New Orleans, and altogether the syndicate controlled more than two thousand miles of coastline.

His man in New York was Frank Yale, the man for whom he had once washed dishes. All worked well until the spring of 1927, when Yale's liquor shipments began to be hijacked. Capone, suspecting a double-cross, sent a spy to New York. When the spy was shot Capone's suspicions were confirmed, and a year later to the very day Frank Yale was machine-gunned down in a New York street. The police questioned Capone, but he had been sunning himself in his Florida villa all the while.

Now Frank Yale had been the New York leader of the Unione Siciliana (recently renamed the Italo-American Union), so revenge was inevitable. His

Above **Al Capone's wreath for Antonio Lombardo.**

Opposite **Corpses of the gangsters killed during the St. Valentine's Day Massacre.**

63

Above **George "Bugs" Moran.**

followers left for Chicago without delay, and on 7th September, 1928, they killed Antonio Lombardo, the Chicago President and Capone's personal friend.

Capone was very upset, and hurried to Chicago to give his friend a funeral of fitting magnificence. He then appointed Pasqualino Lolordo, another of his friends, to the office of President.

But the spiral of killings was by no means over. George "Bugs" Moran was now the leader of the old O'Banion gang, and had long nursed his grievance for the murder of Hymie Weiss. He was frightened of Capone, but now that the king was far away in Florida he could afford to be brave. He made an attempt at reorganizing the alky-cooking business and set up in competition to Capone. Then, in January, 1929, he ordered the death of Pasqualino Lolordo.

Capone's act of vengeance was the most staggeringly violent of any Chicago killing, and for a city with the toll of more than three hundred gang deaths in a few years that is a serious judgment indeed.

On 13th February, 1929, Moran received a telephone call: a consignment of liquor was his for a good price, and he must summon his gang to the warehouse. Greedy at the prospect of such a bargain, Moran obeyed.

But it was a brilliant trap. A police car arrived shortly after seven of Moran's men had opened up the warehouse. There was nothing unusual, nothing to show that it was anything but a routine police search. So the seven men obediently disarmed and stood back against the wall, when suddenly two men appeared from around the corner and opened fire with a machine gun. Without a word the "police" turned on their heels and drove away.

Moran himself was saved; he had been late arriving and had seen the police car. So he had decided to "take a little walk" until the coast was clear. On being questioned by the police he broke the gang code of silence with the bitter words, "Only the Capone gang kills like that."

Chicago was stunned by the brutality of the massacre, and the police determined that this time the killers would not get away. It was a hopeless wish. They made a major breakthrough when they discovered that Frank Yale's killer was also a marksman in the Moran gang massacre (through the use of ballistics, which compared the marks left by bullets and can track them to a particular gun). They even named him – Fred Burke of Egan's Rats, St. Louis – but they could not find him. Their other suspects were all acquitted, one by one.

Capone was in Florida, of course, and by a strange coincidence actually deep in conversation with the Miami District Attorney at the very hour of the massacre. Yet the police had no doubt that he was the key figure in the killing, and they did not intend to forget.

Above **The building in which the St. Valentine's Day Massacre took place.**

"The funeral was a success – seventeen carloads of flowers – a cortège two miles long, twelve pall-bearers in tuxedos – a silk American flag, topped with a brass eagle; a silk Italian flag, topped with a crown and cross; a floral piece, suspended between two trees, bearing the name 'T. Lombardo' in pink and white carnations." *F. D. Pasley. Al Capone.*

15. The Unseating of Capone

Some months after the Moran gang massacre, in May, 1929, Capone went to a mammoth conference of fifty gang chiefs from all the major cities of the United States. It was an impressive gathering, held in the luxury of the President Hotel, Atlantic City, a sort of Vice Kings' Disarmament Conference, in which peace treaties were renewed and, in Capone's words. "Each man signed on the dotted line." They had taken on the formality of a national government, these criminals, and it was tacitly understood who was president.

The climax of Capone's career had been reached, and the turning point was midnight on 16th May, 1929. It was then that he was arrested with his bodyguard, "Slippery" Frank Rio, as they were leaving a cinema in Philadelphia. They were charged with carrying deadly weapons, and the night magistrate made his feelings plain: "My only regret is that you are not before me on charges which would justify me in ridding the United States of you for ever."

The next day Capone was sentenced to a year's imprisonment. It was strange that he had failed to use his protective legal ploys, for he was paying out money all the time for exactly this emergency, so it is possible that he actually wanted to "lie low" for a while. But he was expecting a maximum of three months, and the words "one year" gave him a terrible shock.

> **"I have a wife and eleven-year-old boy I idolize at Palm Island, Florida. If I could go there and forget it all, I would be the happiest man in the world. I want peace, and I'm willing to live and let live."** *Al Capone, just after his arrest in Philadelphia.*

Opposite **The Depression, New York, Christmas, 1931. Hungry men queueing up for a free Christmas dinner at the Municipal Lodging House.**

However his influence did gain him a transfer – to a jail where the discipline was far from rigorous. Here he had a cell with a telephone and easy chairs, and could conduct his business almost as though he were in Florida! He was treated like a celebrity, and the newspapers kept an eager public well informed: "Capone Gains Eleven Pounds," and, "Capone Reads Life of Napoleon". Whether moved by real generosity, or by knowing that publicity followed his every move, he spent no less than $1,000 on crafts made by the prison inmates.

Capone's sentence was reduced to ten months for good behaviour, and the prison Governor obligingly fooled the waiting pressmen by allowing him out ten hours before the official time. In this way he was able to slip into Chicago unnoticed, much to the chagrin of the city police force.

He found the city changed beyond recognition. The Depression had come the previous autumn, throwing three million men out of work and leaving much less money for the bootleg industry. Chicago had especially suffered, for it was discovered that Mayor Thompson and his administration had embezzled a fortune in city funds.

Thompson's business had also been badly hit by the activities of Eliot Ness and "The Untouchables." Ness was a young and ambitious Prohibition agent, and his one aim was to close down all the breweries and distilleries. He used gangster techniques to do this. He built a ten-ton truck with a steel battering ram, and literally burst through the brewery doors and confiscated whatever was inside. As proof of his success during the last six months of Capone's imprisonment he staged a parade, and forty-five confiscated beer trucks were slowly driven beneath Capone's window in the Hotel Lexington.

Capone threw a fit. He smashed two chairs over a table and rushed screaming around the room. But beneath the rage there lay bleak anxiety. He had far from given in, but he had periods of illness, and he was beginning to realize the size of the forces massed against him.

Sensing that the days of bootlegging were almost over, he cleverly devised a new source of income – "racketeering." This was soon to become a favourite among the big crime bosses of America. He took money from the Labour Unions, from trade guilds, and even from employers' associations, in return for a guarantee of "protection" – mainly against his own army of thugs. It brought him a healthy fortune.

But he was under constant attack. The most effective was the Chicago Crime Commission's "public enemy campaign." The Commission had circulated across the nation a list of "public enemies" with the instructions that they be hounded and harassed in every conceivable way. Capone was naturally at the top of the list.

So for the second time in his life he was followed by a train of policemen, and when he left for Florida he found that his house had been padlocked. A tremendous legal battle ensued. Capone's lawyers sought an injunction – a court order to allow him to live in peace in his own home. But the Public Prosecutor replied: "It was just as much a crime to permit Capone to live in Florida, as it would be to allow a rattlesnake to live in a garden where it would bite children." These were amazing words for a court of law, but they showed how far Capone's years of lawlessness had backfired upon him. He was arrested several times, and he fought back by charging the Mayor and other Miami dignitaries with "conspiracy to deprive him of his liberty." He was right, but he had little public sympathy. The legal ping-pong battle continued through the summer, until

"He deserves to die and has no right to live. Capone has become an almost mythical being. He is not a myth, but a reptile who deserves to be crushed."
Judge Lyle, in his address to the Chicago Safety Council, December, 1930.

Capone finally won the right to live in Florida. For the moment he could relax once more, but the lull was not to last for long.

In October 1929, the Wall Street stock market crashed, and Americans of all classes faced bankruptcy, unemployment and poverty. The good times of the Twenties were over; and the luxurious life-style of the big-time criminal, which had once seemed glamorous and exciting, now became a national disgrace. Also public opinion began to see the foolishness of prohibition, which had made the crime-wave respectable. Capone, like any good businessman, had diversified, but bootlegging, the biggest source of easy money, was a declining market. Corruption in city authorities had also become a national scandal, and the gangsters were now up against State and Federal officials who were much harder to bribe or threaten. Gambling, brothel-keeping and protection racketeering went on making big money, but for Al Capone the days of luxury were almost over.

"He has been an ideal prisoner. I cannot estimate the money he has given away. Of course, we cannot inquire where he gets it. He's in the racket. He admits it. But you can't tell me he's all bad, after I've seen him many times a week for ten months, and seen him with his wife and his boy and his mother." *Dr. Goddard of the Pennysylvania State Board of Prison Inspectors, shortly after Capone's release.*

Opposite **Al Capone in the grounds of his home at Palm Island.**

After the long history of gang killings, it seemed almost ironical that the murder of one crime reporter should be a major step in Capone's downfall. Yet so it was.

On 9th June, 1930, while Capone was busy with the Miami courts, Alfred J. Lingle, crime reporter for the Chicago *Tribune*, was killed. His death triggered off a newspaper campaign against gangdom, and the *Tribune* announced that it would not rest until it had found the killers. It hinted that the police were ineffective – and so spurred them on to the most complete investigation they had made so far.

They never found the murderers, but they did un-cover some vital information. It was soon clear that Lingle had been no mere reporter; he had lived like a prince in expensive hotel rooms, operating as a go-between for the gangs and the police department. He had worn one of those diamond belts that Capone gave to friends who helped him. The investigation revealed such evidence of corruption among Chicago officials that a spokesman for the State's Attorney's office remarked, "A lot of men will be leaving town." But, so entrenched was corruption in Chicago, there was no noticeable rush!

The most important discovery of all came when one of the suspects, the Moran gang's accountant Mr. Jack Zuta, was killed on Capone's orders. Capone was

"**The** *Tribune* **accepts this challenge. It is war. There will be casualties, but that is to be expected, it being war. The** *Tribune* **has the support of all other Chicago newspapers . . . Justice will make a fight of it or it will abdicate.**" *The Tribune's answer to what it considered the "challenge" of gangdom in murdering Jake Lingle.*

Opposite **Al Capone, accused of income tax evasion, signing a $50,000 bail bond as two Assistant U.S. Attorneys (right) look on.**

probably not connected with Lingle's death, but the killing of Zuta proved to be a fatal mistake. For Zuta had been a meticulous accountant, and among his private papers the police found a complete record of the takings of the Moran gang. At last they had concrete evidence of the financial operations of the gangs.

The papers were handed over to the tax authorities, who were still mid-way through their enormous dossier on Capone. Capone now had good reason to be worried, for both his brother Ralph and his former business manager, Jack Guzik, were already in prison for tax evasion. He knew that he would be the trump card.

He retreated to Florida, announcing that he had retired. He even missed the splendour of his sister Mafalda's wedding in Chicago, for he had become wary of publicity. "There's a lot of grief attached to the limelight," he remarked in an injured voice. He also risked being arrested in Chicago, for the police had ingeniously brought in a Vagrancy Act. With this they could arrest a "vagrant" (defined as "one without visible means of support"). So if Capone was arrested, he would have to prove his means of support; and there he was trapped, for once he admitted to an income he could be charged for tax evasion.

Capone knew that he was cornered, but he fought with spirit and wit during his court appearances: "While Judge Lyle has been spending thousands of dollars trying to get into office, I have been spending thousands feeding the hungry," he told reporters.

Eventually, on 13th March, 1931, Capone was charged in his absence, at a secret hearing, with evading income tax for 1924. In June he travelled to Chicago to answer an indictment for tax evasion from 1924 until 1929, plus no less than 5,000 violations of the Prohibition laws.

He had offered a bribe of $1,500,000 to "settle out of

court" and he had hired gunmen to intimidate the three-man team of tax investigators, but his old tricks had failed. There was nothing to do but face the music.

He finally stood before the court in a light brown summer suit and perky straw hat, confident that the jury had been paid off by his lawyers, and that the District Attorney had agreed to a maximum sentence of three years in return for a plea of guilty. But to his horror the jury had been changed at the last minute, and the judge announced that he had no intention of being bound by the agreement. He would merely "listen to the recommendations of the District Attorney."

The trial went on for twelve days. Streams of witnesses testified to the sums Capone had spent – tailors, jewellers, butchers, and thousands of Capone's ex-employees. His lawyers claimed that the evidence proved no more than that he was a spendthrift, but an ominous cloud hung over the court. The culmination came on 24th October, when the sentence was delivered: Capone would go to prison for eleven years and pay a $50,000 fine and $30,000 costs.

"I have given orders to the five Deputy Police Commissioners to make this town so quiet that you will be able to hear a consumptive canary cough."
Police Commissioner Russell's statement after the Lingle murder.

Below **Al Capone (left), convicted of income tax evasion, on the train en route to Atlanta prison.**

17. Capone in Prison

Capone was visibly shaken by his sentence, although he tried very hard to smile. Emerging from the courtroom to the sight of waiting press cameras, he momentarily lost control. White with rage, he grabbed at a bucket of water to throw over the press photographers, but was pulled back by the guards. He spent the night in the courthouse jail, scorning the supper on a tin plate and refusing to see the press, apparently blaming them for his long sentence.

He felt stung by the blow, and by what he saw as public ingratitude. "All I ever did was sell beer and whisky to our best people," he claimed. "All I ever did was supply a demand that was pretty popular. I have never heard of anyone getting more than five years for income tax trouble, but they are prejudiced against me. I never had a chance."

True, the court had dealt with more than Capone the tax-evader. They had also judged Al Capone the bootlegger, the murderer, the king of crime and the man who had insolently escaped them on so many charges for so long.

Six months later, having been refused the right to appeal, Capone was transported to Atlanta jail. This time he was pleased by the flashing press cameras, for he had missed publicity – "Jeez, you'd think Mussolini was passin' through!"

Above **Mae Capone, wife of Al Capone.**

Opposite **Al Capone (centre) being led to the train which carried him to Atlanta prison.**

"Alcatraz is a jail of eternal silence. No prisoner may speak except during one authorized period a week, from one to three-thirty on Saturday. It's enough to drive you crazy. Even hard guys like Capone are furious at the silence, at the strict discipline and at the harsh punishment."
A released Alcatraz prisoner, interviewed in April, 1935.

Left **Alcatraz.**

He became prisoner No. 40866 at Atlanta Penitentiary, and had to work cutting out prison overalls for $7 a month. In April, 1932, he once again hit the newspaper headlines. The baby son of the world famous aviator, Charles Lindbergh, had been kidnapped, and Capone offered to hunt down the kidnappers if he could be freed. His younger brother would enter jail as hostage until his return. But the authorities replied with an emphatic "no."

In August, 1934, he was sent to the new top security prison of Alcatraz, a tiny, rocky island in San Francisco bay. In Atlanta his life had been tolerable; he had shared a cell with an old friend from his New York days, his family had visited once a month, and he had received piles of fan mail. But Alcatraz was very different. It was a special prison for the dangerous criminal, totally cut off from outside life, and Capone was bitterly offended by his transfer.

The discipline was harsh, but Capone refused to join in the prisoners' strikes because he was anxious to shorten his sentence for good behaviour. This made many of the prisoners resent him and in June, 1936, he was badly wounded when one of them stabbed him with a pair of scissors.

One day he stumbled into the prison canteen, deathly pale and chattering incoherently. He was found to be suffering from syphilis, a venereal disease which, unless treated in its early stages, does permanent damage to the brain and is eventually fatal. He was hurriedly sent to San Pedro prison for medical observation, and suffered periodic mental attacks.

He was released on 17th November, 1939, and his health recovered a little – although the headlines announced "Capone Dying." The government sued him for more arrears of tax, and he made a final settlement in 1942. This apart, he lived a quiet life with his

> "He behaves so well in Atlanta that the other inmates are beginning to think he is a milk-sop. He had been trying unsuccessfully to get a place in the prison baseball team. He is a model prisoner, and obeys every order the second it is given."
> *United States Attorney Dwight Green, after a visit to Atlanta, December,* 1932.

family in Florida, hidden from the public eye. He read occasionally, and loved to talk with Sonny, but his speech grew slurred and his mind increasingly wandered.

His death came on the morning of 25th January, 1947, at the age of forty-eight. His family rushed to be at his bedside – not only Sonny and Mae, but also his mother, three of his brothers, and his favourite sister, Mafalda. His last years had been so quiet that his death was hardly noticed by the world at large.

It seemed impossible to believe that his great fortune, estimated at $25,000,000 in 1930, had been entirely eaten away. Yet so his lawyers claimed: "He died penniless," they told the incredulous tax authorities, and certainly Mae and Sonny both went to work to make a living. So whether or not he managed to keep one final trick up his sleeve, a last defiance of the government, no-one will ever know.

> "I've been made an issue and I'm not complaining. But why don't they go after all these bankers who took the savings of the thousands of poor people and lost them in bank failures. How about that?" *Al Capone, just before going to Atlanta Penitentiary.*

Below **Mourners at Al Capone's burial service.**

18. Capone the History Maker

Al Capone was the first and only real hero-gangster. Before him the gang leaders had operated in the underworld, unseen by the public. Since his downfall the big crime bosses have known better than to come out in the open, and court publicity. They work secretly, fronted by some legal business. But Capone played handsomely to the public. He gave them a grand spectacle, touring the town like a king in his limousine, handing out presents, adoring publicity. He was a symbol of success and he allowed them to share it.

It is not hard to understand how he came to be admired by many Chicagoans of the 1920s. A sociologist from the University of Chicago said: "I couldn't look upon the gangs of the Prohibition period as criminals. The people of Chicago wanted booze, gambling and women, and the Capone organization was a public utility supplying the customers with what they wanted."

Capone himself had similar thoughts: "I'm a public benefactor . . . You can't cure thirst by law. They call me a bootlegger. Yes. It's bootleg while it's on the trucks, but when your host hands it to you on a silver plate, it's hospitality. What's Al done then? He's supplied a legitimate demand. Some call it bootlegging, say I violate the Prohibition law – who doesn't?"

Since so many of the politicians were corrupt, and

"If people didn't want beer and wouldn't drink it, a fellow would be crazy for going round trying to sell it. I've seen gambling houses, too, in my travels, and I never saw anyone point a gun at a man and make him go in. I never heard of anyone being forced to go to a place to have some fun." *Al Capone.*

Opposite **Al Capone pictured as he was leaving Alcatraz.**

there were men like Mayor Thompson who drank alcohol, accepted bribes and embezzled public funds, it is hardly surprising that the gangster was not generally regarded as a creature of evil. The government did little to help the poor, but Capone opened the first soup kitchens during the Depression, giving free food to more than 3,000 unemployed each day. He was probably the first gangster ever to run a social aid programme.

He was also a pioneer, the first man to turn crime into an organized business empire. In ten years he had risen from the slums to a status that was unique in its power and scope; he was a multi-millionaire, he controlled a national business enterprise, and he more or less governed the politics of Chicago. None of his successors in the crime world have ever enjoyed this amount of power.

He taught them how to build a business, logically and thoroughly. He had first taken over his home city, then the suburbs, then the State of Illinois. Then he had spread slowly across the country until by the Atlantic City conference of 1929 he could lay down national terms and price-fixing agreements with complete confidence that they would be obeyed. Even one of his tax investigators called him a brilliant businessman, adding regretfully, "if only he had turned his mind to something legal . . ."

He taught them other lessons, too. He paved the way for the business of racketeering (which has since made many a fortune), and showed them the need for political allies. Owing to his mistakes his successors are now careful to remain anonymous, to avoid publicity, and not to meddle openly in politics, and they are also very prompt in paying their taxes. Being unseen, they represent a far greater problem than Capone ever did.

What should have killed the public's admiration for

Capone was his methods. Murder, violence and intimidation cannot be justified, though many a gangster thought otherwise. The Sicilian for instance, with his heritage of blood-feuds and loyalty to the death, for him this was a way of life, and the only way he knew. But Capone, although he was born in the immigrant slums and grew up in the vicious gangworld of New York, did not kill out of a sense of honour. For him it was a business proposition and the best way to stamp out competition.

And here again Capone was an innovator. He had successfully adapted the old spirit of the Mafia into the business life of America, he had modernized the gang set-up so that it was no more a game of petty crime in the back streets, but efficient "Big Business without top hats." He had used gang emotions (jealousy and loyalty) to stop business competition. He had started something that is still, regrettably, very deep-rooted in the America of today.

Capone is a difficult person to summarize. He was a hero and a villain – always an irresistable combination. He *was* the Chicago of the 1920s, he made that piece of history, and he will never be forgotten. It has in fact been prophesied that Al Capone's name in the distant future will be romanticised like that of many a pirate king.

"He cannot be summarized by all the conventional terms of disapproval, that he was evil, ruthless or corrupt, although he was, after all, a pioneer of a kind, for nobody before had done quite what he did, and in him there were undoubted qualities of imagination, forcefulness and ingenuity." *Kenneth Allsop. The Bootleggers.*

Left **Al Capone's mausoleum at Mt. Olivet Cemetry, Chicago.**

Principal Characters

Aiello, Joseph. Leader of the Sicilian Aiello gang, and Capone's chief rival during 1927. Killed in 1930.

O'Banion, Dion (1892–1924). Powerful leader of an Irish gang whose aim was to destroy the authority of the Italians (especially Capone and Torrio). A gangster by night and a florist during the day.

O'Donnell, Spike. Leader of an Irish gang, and the first challenger of Capone and Torrio. His old-fashioned methods of gang warfare made him an easy victim.

Genna, Angelo. Leader of the Sicilian Genna gang, and eldest of the six Genna brothers. A fierce rival of Capone, ambitious to be President of the Unione Siciliana, killed in 1925.

Guzik, Jack (1886–1956). The accountant and "financial wizard" of Capone's organization. Imprisoned briefly for tax evasion, and died peacefully in his bed at the age of 70.

Lombardo, Antonio. Born in Sicily and emigrated to the United States in 1910. A staunch ally of Capone, and President of the Unione Siciliana from January, 1926, until his assassination in 1928.

Moran, George "Bugs" (1892–1957). An Irishman with a criminal record from 1910 onwards. A rival of Capone in 1928, when he became leader of the old O'Banion gang, he narrowly escaped death in the

St. Valentine's Day Massacre. Thereafter most of his life was spent in prison, where he died at the age of 65.

Ness, Eliot (1903–1957). Prohibition agent who successfully closed many breweries in 1929–1930. He became president of a paper company after the repeal of the Prohibition law.

Thompson, William Hale (1869–1944). Son of a rich landowner and a keen sportsman. At first reluctant to enter politics, but he soon enjoyed the publicity and ruled Chicago with corruption and inefficiency. Mayor of Chicago from 1917–1923, and 1927–1930.

Torrio, John (1864–1939). Went to Chicago in 1919 and built up a powerful crime organization by 1920, when he recruited Al Capone. Retired from Chicago gang-life in 1925, and became National Head of the Unione Siciliana after Frank Yale's death in 1928.

Yale, Frank, National head of the Unione Siciliana. From 1926 in charge of the New York shipments in Capone's national network, murdered in 1928 on Capone's orders because he had double-crossed him.

Table of Dates

1928	Capone buys his villa on Palm Island, Miami Beach. The authorities start to investigate his activities, seeking evidence of tax evasion. The Pineapple Primary. Frank Yale is killed in New York by Capone's men. Antonio Lombardo, President of the Unione Siciliana, is assassinated.
1929	The St. Valentine's Day Massacre. Capone attends the Atlantic City conference. Capone is sent to jail for nine months, charged with carrying dangerous weapons.
1930	Chicago is declared to be $300,000,000 in debt "due to the mismanagement of Thompson and his friends." Capone is released from jail. Crime reporter Jake Lingle is murdered.
1931	"Big Bill" Thompson is defeated by Anton J. Cernak in the Mayorial election in Chicago. Capone is sentenced to eleven years' imprisonment for tax evasion.
1932	Franklyn D. Roosevelt is elected President of the United States.
1933	Prohibition officially ends when Utah becomes the 36th State to ratify its repeal.
1934	Capone is transferred to Alcatraz.
1939	Capone is released.
1947	Capone dies.

Glossary

ALKY-COOKING   Making alcohol with the use of chemicals.

CRAPS   A gambling game played with dice.

THE DEPRESSION   An economic disaster. In America the public invested too much money in industry, and because agricultural prices had been falling since 1926 there was no background capital to support this. On 24th October, 1929, thirteen million shares were sold on Wall Street, credit failed, and one by one the banks crashed. Millions of people lost all their savings, and unemployment soared throughout the following winter.

DIVE   A type of night club where the clientèle is (usually) from the underworld.

FEDORA   A hat with a crown and a wide brim.

INDICTMENT   A formal accusation, or criminal charge.

INJUNCTION   A court order which either restrains someone from doing a wrongful act, or compels them to do a rightful one (such as restore property to its rightful owner).

LIQUOR BOSS   The man who controlled the distribution of alcohol.

THE MAFIA   A secret society which originated in Sicily, and to which only Sicilians can belong. It has its own laws, and its own code of "omerta", by which all members swear to remain utterly loyal to the society and to keep the seal of silence on all its activities. The penalty for breaking any of the laws is death. The Mafia ruled Sicily during the nineteenth century, and although Benito Mussolini tried to crush it in the 1920s, it is still influential in politics and business. In America it grew to control many illegal activities, such as smuggling, traffic in narcotics, kidnapping and labour racketeering, and there too, it entered the world of politics. It is unhappily still very active.

RED-LIGHT DISTRICT Brothels usually had red lights in their front windows, or over their entrances. The sector of a city where brothels and gambling dens were found is therefore known as the red-light district.

PAROLE A prisoner is parolled when he is freed on condition that he promises to keep a record of good behaviour.

ROUGHNECK A thug, or violent person.

SEDAN A saloon car.

SLOUCH HAT A hat with part of the brim turned down, similar to the English trilby.

SMALL-TIMER A businessman operating on his own, with no powerful organization behind him.

SOCIOLOGIST Person who studies the development and laws of human society.

SPEAKEASY A bar selling illegal alcohol, now simply a bar.

TUXEDO A dinner jacket.

Index